How to Pass
GRADUATE
RECRUITMENT
TESTS

How to Pass GRADUATE RECRUITMENT TESTS

Psychometric Tests Used in Graduate and Management Recruitment

Mike Bryon

KOGAN
PAGE

First published in 1994, entitled *Graduate Recruitment Tests*.
Reprinted 1994, title changed to *How to Pass Recruitment Tests*.

Kogan Page Limited
120 Pentonville Road
London N1 9JN

© Mike Bryon 1994

British Library Cataloguing in Publication Data

A CIP record for this book is available from the British Library.

ISBN 0-7494-0994-0

Typeset by DP Photosetting, Aylesbury, Bucks
Printed and bound in Great Britain by
Clays Ltd, St Ives plc

Contents

Acknowledgements

I am grateful to Gino Fox and Katy Shay for comments on Chapter 4 and whose contributions led to improvements in substance and saved several mistakes.

My greatest debt is to my partner, Kirsten, who provided indispensable support in the development of the practice questions in English usage and who also helped to improve my English after reading a first draft.

This book is dedicated to Hope, born 3 August 1993, whose delivery fittingly coincided with the despatch of the manuscript to the publisher.

Preface

During the 1990s, as in no previous decade, job prospects began to look bleak for graduates and managers, and competition for jobs led many employers to raise their entry standards.

Psychometric tests are widely used in graduate and management recruitment. Large organisations tend to attract many hundreds or even thousands of applicants and rely on these tests as a cost-effective way to reduce the number of candidates.

It is common for job-seekers to take measures to improve their CV and to undertake interview practice. However, relatively few seek to improve their performance in the employers' tests. The aspects of these tests with which most candidates have difficulty are the arithmetic and English usage sections. It may have been some years since the candidate was trained in these subjects – in many cases they would not have been tested in them since their GCSEs. Many will have become dependent on calculators, the use of which is not allowed in the majority of admission tests, and the grammar classes at school are often a distant and hazy memory.

This book provides advice and practice exercises relevant to many of the tests used by employers to recruit managers and graduates. The practice exercises are intended to allow you to build up speed, accuracy and confidence. Both a maths and a grammar glossary are provided to enable you to revise the rules of arithmetic and English usage. Advice is also provided on the type and amount of practice which you should undertake. Answers to all the practice questions are provided at the end of each chapter.

Chapter 1
Selection Tests – There is No Getting Away From Them

The paper and pen tests used by employers to allocate staff are attributed with a surprising range of titles. 'Selection', 'psychometric',* 'competency' and 'aptitude' are just a few of the descriptions used. It is not even safe to call them paper and pen tests as increasingly they are carried out on computer terminals.

It is estimated that over 70 per cent of the UK's top companies use tests in the recruitment of managers and graduates. As well as an aid during recruitment, these tests are put to an array of other uses. For example, a local authority in Greater London recently used competency tests to select staff for redundancy. Even if you seek to improve your career prospects through higher education, you may still face them. In this context, the best-known example is the GMAT (General Management Attainment Test) – the entry qualification for top stream MBA courses. Worldwide, over 200,000 people take the GMAT each year.

The pseudo-scientific view of selection tests

If you face the GMAT, the Civil Service graduate entrance exam, one of the numerous battery of tests and assessments used during management or graduate selection, or even a set of tests to decide whether or not you are to be made redundant, then a lot may depend on how well you score on the day.

---

* 'Psychometric tests' attempt to quantify performance in numbers. The term is used when a test provides a numerical measurement of the extent to which an individual possesses a particular trait or set of traits.

Unfortunately, few candidates realise that they can significantly improve their scores. It is all too often falsely assumed that your score is determined purely by the extent to which you inherently either possess or lack certain aptitudes. In this way the test is seen in a detached, clinical way of classifying you (as a blood test can classify your blood type) as either possessing or lacking the necessary aptitude.

Such a pseudo-scientific view of selection testing is not only false but is a view which will serve you badly. Taking a selection test is not a matter of rolling up your sleeve and putting up with the discomfort of the needle while the scientist takes his or her sample. It is important you realise that you have considerable influence over your test performance and that hard work, determination and, most of all, systematic preparation, can lead to a considerable improvement in your score.

It is not only the test candidate who has suffered the specious effects of the pseudo-scientific view. While it has led test candidates to be fatalistic about their likely score, it has also led test authors and administrators to be rather ambivalent on the issue of coaching.

Test authors and administrators have a tendency to view coaching as a challenge to the validity of their tests. Some go as far as to deny that any significant improvement in score can be gained from practice. They are wrong; and, again, the error is born of the view that tests afford a pseudo-scientific classification of a candidate's aptitude. Subscribers to this school of thought would assure us that a test distinguishes categorically between those with and those without the potential to do a job. Coaching creates a problem with this view because the validity of the test starts to look rather questionable when someone can, following a few hours' practice, be transformed from supposedly not having the potential for the job, to possessing it.

The historical origins of the pseudo-scientific view of tests

Historically, test authors have tried to produce tests which examine in the candidate a set of qualities which are not subject to cultural bias or the variance of particular occupations. These tests promised to investigate a set of qualities which were relevant to a multitude of occupations and cultures and measured an individual's potential regardless of the context. The idea of intelligence is closely bound up with this kind of approach.

In fact, claims made by early test authors suffered as a result of naive views on the connection between intelligence, criminality and morality. In the years leading up to World War 1, exponents of testing made a series of ambitious claims for the contribution testing could make towards the ordering of society. Supposedly, mental measurement through testing could be used to predict whether you would succeed in higher education, be suitable for a particular career or be law-abiding.

These were heady days: the days for believing it was possible to adopt a universal language such as Esperanto. So why not a universal test which measured potential, ability or aptitude, irrespective of where you were in the world, the lifestyle you led or your background?

These were also times when racism and racist views were prominent. The new science of testing was heralded as a way of identifying genetic differences, and correlations were made between test score and race. During World War 1, the American Army tested almost 2 million recruits. After the war, studies of these results emphasised the differences in the scores attained by different races and these results were used to promote, among many things, racist immigration policies.

It is now widely recognised that these racist conclusions were false. It was later shown that a score in the army test had a strong correlation with the length of time the candidate had spent at school and their length of residency in the United States. The most recent immigrants and the poorest sections of society (who could not afford to educate their children) largely belonged to particular races and, therefore, obtained the lowest scores. When these factors were taken into account, it became clear that the claims made about racial differences were untrue and that the test had merely identified the effects of a racist education system and had discriminated against the most recent immigrants.

This, unfortunately, is the heritage of modern selection tests. This is not to say that there were not responsible followers of 'the new science' and certainly, the test which you are likely to sit will not be used to make racist claims. However, from these controversial origins, the modern test evolved and a multi-million pound and, in particular, a multi-million dollar industry arose.

Exorcising the pseudo-scientific view

If you face a selection test it is essential you approach it with the right mental attitude. In particular, you must realise that your score can be improved by your own efforts. To do this I propose to review what I have called 'dogmas' of selection tests. If you are reading this book as someone who uses tests in recruitment then your organisation can only benefit if you realise that the tests you use have significant limitations.

Dogma 1
That tests measure fixed and predetermined aptitudes

Aptitude is defined as a natural tendency or propensity, a natural capacity for a particular pursuit. Many of the difficulties with this notion arise because aptitude is often taken as something fixed at birth and not open to revision. The idea of a fixed and predetermined aptitude has held considerable influence over western culture. It is an influence which can be traced back to the writings of the ancient Greeks. Plato, in *The Republic*, a classic text of ancient Greek philosophy, wrote: '. . . when god fashioned you, he added gold in the composition of those of you who are qualified to be rulers; he put silver in the auxiliaries; and iron and bronze in the farmers and the rest.'

If we take this quote literally, and Plato only used the analogy as what he called a myth, then from birth it would seem that it is already predetermined whether or not we have the potential to, for example, rule or farm. All that is needed is a test to establish which metal our composition contains and education and occupation could be allocated in a very effective manner.

However, this view ignores any contribution made by upbringing, education or training. Without getting too embroiled in the nature/nurture debate, most people would agree that nurture has a significant contribution to make towards, for example, a person's capacity to undertake a particular occupation. What is more, adult training and mature student entry into higher education has demonstrated that people can successfully change career at any age. The individual who views a test as a measure of aptitude which is fixed and not open to revision risks underestimating their own potential and the potential of their staff.

Dogma 2
That tests are objective in the same way as the natural sciences

Test authors and publishers go to considerable lengths to reassure us that their tests are objective and reliable and that they afford the selection of candidates with the potential to succeed in the given career or position. However, tests are only objective and reliable if compared with other recruitment and selection methods, such as interviews, which are denounced as unreliable. When test authors talk about the objectivity of these tests they mean that the test may be, for example, three times more reliable than interviews for predicting job performance. It is essential we realise that three times more reliable than unreliable still remains qualitatively different from the objectivity attained in the natural sciences.

Reconsider the case of the blood type test. There is no doubt or ambiguity attached to a blood type classification; there is very little prospect of it changing given different circumstances such as the day on which the sample is taken. Yet the objectivity of selection tests is quantifiably different. They are, at best, only indicators of potential. Had you *not* been suffering from a cold, had you been more familiar with the test conditions, less nervous, better practised in mental arithmetic, not made that silly mistake ... then you may have been classified differently. You may have passed something you otherwise failed. Selection tests lack the objectivity associated with the natural sciences. This is because you, the subject, have considerable influence over the outcome. It is also the case because the measurement of job performance is, itself, subjective.*

Dogma 3
That tests afford the selection of the 'best' candidate

Tests are scored and, of course, some candidates score higher than others. There is a tendency among recruiters to assume that the higher a candidate scores the greater that candidate's potential. Equally common is the tendency for the recruiter to be relieved that the poor scoring candidate has been identified in such a dramatic and clear-cut way. For a recruiter there is something very reassuring about a test score.

This view is perfectly understandable. Imagine if you had to select from 900 candidates five with whom you were going to have to work and achieve the targets set by your line manager. You would, naturally, want to select the best and the test score would appear the most unambiguous indication of potential at a time when all else seemed relative.

However, tests impose constraints on the candidate. There is only one, or a few, acceptable ways in which a candidate can successfully approach a question. In effect, the test seeks out and rewards the candidate who knows the system and who has mastered the key skills tested.

How we manage to do our job is not important. What is important is that we do it and do it well. Yet selection tests cannot make this distinction. Under the strict time constraint of the test, where you only pass if you conduct yourself in a particular way, you do not have the opportunity to be creative in your approach. Alternative ways of conducting yourself in the workplace are excluded by the artificial constraints of the

---

* To have a test which is valid, it is important you have a clear set of criteria against which to assess job performance. However, in the case of the majority of jobs it is very difficult to define an unambiguous set of criteria against which job performance can be judged.

test. The best scoring candidate, therefore, may not turn out to have the best performance in the job.

If you rely too heavily on test scores, as many employers do, you risk failing to recognise the potential for creativity and the ability of people to develop new strategies. By attributing too great an importance to the score of a candidate, recruiters are often encouraged to take the view that candidate x is the best and candidate y the second best and so on. Tests by their very nature attribute to the workplace a far too simplistic set of performance indicators and they are intolerant of alternative ways of working and solving problems. Recruiters who ignore this risk paying a high price in business efficiency.

Towards a more healthy perspective

There is a world of difference between the professional and responsible users of selection tests and a regrettable minority of malpractitioners. Increasingly, employers are adopting a more balanced view as to the contribution tests can make towards a fair and equitable selection process. These days it is increasingly common for tests to be viewed as predictors of job performance rather than some ultimate arbitrator of aptitude. There are other encouraging changes taking place in the attitude expressed by employers (and test authors) towards tests.

A welcome change is the shift away from the abstract towards exercises more relevant to the workplace. Increasingly, employers are using tests which are more closely associated with the demands of the job. The vocabulary tested is often taken from the workplace and the examples and exercises are increasingly adapted tasks taken directly from the job.

A second change is a recognition that tests may not provide a definitive classification but one which is conditional and subject to circumstance. Test publishers talk openly about the need for a 'broad-based assessment process' which includes tests, personality questionnaires, group exercises and interview. Theorists in recruitment strategy talk of the advantages of a diverse array of routes into employment.

17

Most important of all, realise that tests produce a classification which can be influenced by you, the approach you take and the amount of preparation which you undertake.

Chapter 2

The Maximum Benefit of Practice

How much will practice help?

Everyone, if they practise, could improve their test score. The interesting question is whether or not they can improve their score sufficiently to pass something they would have otherwise failed?

Practice most benefits the candidate who is otherwise likely to fail by only a few marks; such people are sometimes referred to as 'near miss candidates'. The near miss candidate benefits most from practice because it is almost certain to ensure that she/he passes.

Candidates who have little or no experience of employers' tests can, through practice, demonstrate a quite considerable improvement in their score. The biggest gains are achieved quickly and then the rate of improvement slows. Figure 2.1 illustrates the likely rate of improvement over 25 hours for a candidate new to tests.

If you have recently left higher education much of what you studied will have prepared you for the tests used by employers. As a result of this preparation, it may be that you will not demonstrate the kind of improvement indicated in Figure 2.1. However, you may still benefit from practice. Employers' tests often require the candidate to undertake tests in arithmetic or English usage, subjects which you may not have studied for some years. The manner in which the questions are posed is also likely to be unfamiliar and practice will help you to realise the test demands. Finally, practice will allow you to deal with any nervousness and help you to avoid common mistakes.

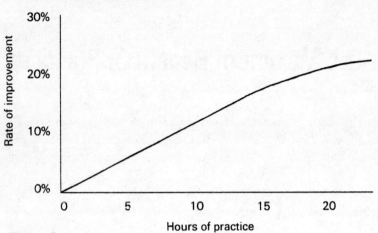

Figure 2.1

What kind of practice?

It is essential that the material on which you practise is similar to the questions which occur in the real test. The employer should have sent you a description of the test with examples of the types of question which comprise the real test. Study this document carefully and seek out practice questions which closely resemble the questions in the real test.

Two types of practice should be undertaken if the maximum benefit is to be gained. You should:

1. Practise without time constraint and in an informal, relaxed situation on questions similar to those which occur in the real test. The aim of this kind of practice is that you realise the demands of the questions, understand how to approach them and gain speed and confidence in your ability to answer them.

2. Practise on realistic questions against a strict time constraint and under realistic test conditions. Ideally, you should practise on mock tests. The aim of this type of practice is that you get used to answering the questions under the time constraints and conditions of the test. This kind of practice helps you to avoid mistakes which result from the pressure of the situation. You should aim to practise on a minimum of three realistic mock tests.

If you are unable to obtain practice tests make some up for yourself. Seek out approximately 40 realistic questions; much of the practice material provided in this book may be suitable. Allow yourself 45 seconds a question (in a real test it is unusual that you are able to complete all the questions in the time allowed). Make sure that all sections of the real test are represented. If, for example, the real test comprises sub-tests in maths, English usage and business judgement, make sure your practice tests include all three types of question.

How much practice?

Aim to undertake a minimum of 12 hours' practice. If you can obtain sufficient practice material, undertake up to 20 hours. Ensure that you practise right up to the date of your test. Your schedule of work should look something like this:

Hours

1 Study the test description sent to you by the employer	2 Seek out similar questions	3 Seek out similar questions	4 Go through practice questions at your own pace
5 Go through practice questions at your own pace	6 Set yourself a mock test against a strict time-limit	7 Go over the mock test checking the answers	8 Go through practice questions at your own pace
9 Set yourself a second mock test against a strict time-limit	10 Carefully go over the mock test questions	11 Go through practice questions at your own pace	12 Set yourself a third mock test

A summary of research findings on the issue of practice

In order that you might better plan your practice prior to taking an employer's test and make your own assessment as to the likely benefit, consider some of the principal issues believed to determine the value of practice.

An examination of some of the literature on selection tests identified the following findings on the subject of practice:

- Individuals with incomplete educational backgrounds are likely to benefit most from coaching
- Those who have no, or little, previous experience of tests show a rise about twice as large as those who have taken tests before
- Improvements in scores are obtained by experiencing materials similar to those occurring in the real test
- Practice with similar materials under test conditions produces the best results
- Most of the improvement is gained quickly; then the rate of improvement slows
- The effect of coaching is highly specific in that there is little transfer to other types of test
- Big individual differences in coaching are found
- Greatest improvement in test performance is obtained not from coaching but from education
- Graduates who have not studied maths or English language since their GCSEs can significantly improve their test score through practice.

Chapter 3
Great Candidate –
Except for the Maths!

Employers increasingly want all-round recruits. However, many students leave higher education having not studied maths since they were 16. Many applicants to graduate or managerial positions are unable to do basic calculations without using a calculator; yet calculators are not allowed in the majority of selection tests. Research indicates that one in six graduates lack confidence in the use of percentages, averages and the interpretation of tabulated data. Many lack a sufficient command of basic mental arithmetic because of too great a dependence on calculators and poor teaching at school.

In most cases the problem is not innumeracy but a lack of speed and accuracy. The candidate is able to answer the questions but completes too few in the time allowed or makes too many avoidable mistakes.

The majority of applicants need to build up speed, revise forgotten rules and improve accuracy in order to show their true potential. The only way you are going to do this is through practice. It is boring, it is painful even, but it has to be done if you want to pass the test.

There are some very good numeracy textbooks on sale. In recent years the quality has improved considerably. If you need more practice questions than are provided in this book, most bookshops or libraries will stock examples. Space has not allowed me to explain all the various calculations. If you do require illumination, then, again, I would stress the value of some of the excellent books available. Alternatively, ask a friend to explain the methods and set you practice examples. Note, however, that if your helper was taught a different method it is probably best if you do not try to learn the alternative approach, as this usually ends up with you becoming confused.

This section comprises three parts: a diagnostic exercise which is intended to allow you to identify the extent to which you need to practise, a glossary of the key terms which occur in maths tests, and practice questions. For practice in the interpretation of tabulated data see Chapter 5.

In the next few pages you will find 27 questions. Allow yourself 20 minutes in which to complete them. Do not turn the page until you are ready to start. Work as quickly and accurately as you can. Do not use a calculator.

Part 1
A diagnostic exercise

Addition

1. Find the sum of 79004, 24, 325 and 647.

Answer

2. A company representative submits a travel claim form comprising the following:

Monday	105 miles
Tuesday	43 miles
Wednesday	87 miles
Thursday	144 miles
Friday	12 miles

What is the total number of miles?

Answer

3. A study of a family's expenditure found that each week on average it spent the following: £38.60 on food, £57.00 on accommodation, £14.20 on entertainment, £18.70 on heat and light and £9.00 on clothing. Excluding entertainment, what is the total spent?

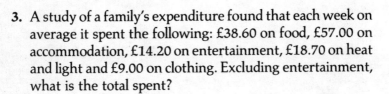

Answer

Subtraction

4. What is the difference between 373 and 3298?

Answer

5. Subtract 10303 from 60002.

Answer

6. The period sales figures for your department are illustrated in the table against your targets. How many unit sales must you make in the last period in order to achieve your overall target?

Period	Sales actual	Targets
1	24	30
2	13	20
3	17	22
4	20	22
5	19	22
6		20

Answer

Multiplication

7. Multiply 35 by 68.

Answer

8. A buyer agrees to pay 16 pence per unit for a lot which totals 103 units. What was the total cost of the purchase? Express your answer in pounds and pence.

Answer

9. A machine can operate at 120 revolutions per minute. How many times will it rotate in half an hour?

Answer

Division of whole numbers

10. Divide 185 by 5.

Answer

11. Divide 2115 by 9.

Answer

12. British Gas send out 27 million bills a year. They have made a deal with the Royal Mail who deliver the bills for £2,700,000. How much does it cost British Gas to deliver each bill?

Answer

Fractions

13. $\dfrac{1}{3} + \dfrac{2}{9} + \dfrac{7}{12} =$

Answer

14. $3\dfrac{5}{8} - 1\dfrac{3}{4} =$

Answer

15. A railway wagon carries $20\frac{1}{8}$ metric tons of flour in $12\frac{1}{2}$ kg bags. How many bags of flour can be loaded on to the wagon? (Note that a metric tone = 1,000 kg.)

Answer

Decimals

16. Convert $\frac{1}{16}$ into decimals.

Answer

17. Multiply 3.7 by 4.83.

Answer

18. The Royal Constabulary employed 2,200 constables in 1993. This figure was projected to fall by 1.2% in 1994. How many constables are projected to be employed in 1994? Express your answer to the nearest whole number.

Answer

Ratios

19. Parked in a street there are 14 cars and 4 motor cycles. What is the ratio of cars to motor cycles?

Answer

20. The ratio of car drivers to cyclists in a city is found to be 4:1. How many cyclists were counted in the survey if the sample totalled 2,500?

Answer

21. A fuel mixture comprises the ratio 14 parts fuel to 1 part oil. How much oil will be present in 9 litres of fuel mixture? (Note there are 100 cl in 1 litre.)

Answer

Averages

22. Find the average of 7, 12, 14 and 16.

Answer

23. A shop sold 3 watches at £16, a ring at £30 and 4 travelling alarm clocks at £9. What was the average sale price?

Answer

24. To pass an exam you have to average 60 marks across four papers. After three papers a candidate's score is averaging 52. What mark must the candidate achieve in the final paper in order to pass the exam?

Answer

Percentages

25. Find 43% of £5.

Answer

26. A pair of shoes is normally priced at £37. What will be the sale price if a 25% discount is offered?

Answer

27. An invoice totals £5000 and includes VAT at 17.5%. How much was the invoice made out for excluding VAT? Round your answer up to the nearest penny.

Answer

You will find the answers to the diagnostic exercises at the end of this chapter. Use this exercise to establish in which types of question you need to undertake further practice.

If you failed to complete the exercise in the suggested time you need more practice in order to increase your speed.

Part 2
Glossary

Key terms and methods

If it is some years since you studied mathematics, then it is important that you remind yourself of the meaning of the key terms and familiarise yourself with the key methods.

Below you will find a glossary of terms, illustrated, where appropriate, with recommended methods. The definitions are intended only as a reminder. The suggested methods are by no means the only way to approach the calculations. I have included a copy of the multiplication tables so that you can seek out patterns, for ease of memory, and relearn them so that you can operate effectively without the aid of a calculator.

All the entries occur in employer tests. Make sure that, before you take a selection test which includes a maths subtest, you can operate quickly, accurately and with confidence the following methods, rules and terms:

Addition

To add positive and negative numbers. If both numbers have a positive or a negative sign add them together and use the same sign in your answer.

If they have different signs then apply the rule that:

$$+ \ - \text{ is the same as } -$$

Remember that if you subtract a smaller number from a larger one the answer will be positive. If you subtract a larger number from a smaller one the result will be negative. For example:

$$2 + -6 = -4$$
$$16 + -2 = 14$$

Algebra

In algebra, letters are used to express general rules of arithmetic. It is a large subject which is complicated at the higher levels. Many selection tests, however, require only basic algebra and it is important that you realise the advantage in speed which simple (or linear) equations can afford.

Practice question

A receiver has to share a sum of money unequally between three creditors. Creditor X is to receive £1000 more than creditor Y. Creditor Z is to receive three times as much as creditor Y. Try to devise a linear equation which allows you to establish how much creditor X will receive if creditor Z is paid £1800. Your equation should allow you to establish that creditor X is paid £1600.

Answer

$$X = \frac{1800}{3} + 1000$$

Angle

Angles are measured in degrees and record the amount of turn. A right angle has 90 degrees, an acute angle less than 90 degrees, an obtuse angle is greater than 90 but less than 180 degrees and a reflex angle is greater than 180 degrees. Angles on a straight line add up to 180 degrees, while angles from a point add up to 360 degrees.

Area

Area is a two-dimensional measurement. To work out the area of a square you multiply the length of one side by itself. All areas are measured in squares, eg square centimetres or square inches. To establish the area of a rectangle you multiply length by width. The area occupied by a triangle is established by multiplying its height by half the length of its base line.

Average

The average or arithmetic mean is found by adding up all the figures and dividing the total by the number of figures.

'Average' differs from 'Mode': the item of data which occurs the most often, and 'Median': the figure or item of data which is in the middle once all the items have been put in a specific order.

Bar chart

A visual representation of data which allows the viewer to make comparisons between the frequency or quantity of items. It is used when the horizontal scale is simply a list. The bars are of equal width; the frequency or quantity is illustrated by the height of the bar.

Brackets

When there appear several ways in which to proceed with a calculation, to ensure that appropriate parts are worked out first they are enclosed within brackets. Always work out the parts in brackets first. Brackets are sometimes referred to as a 'first priority'. A 'second priority' is multiplication and division which must be done before the 'third priority' – addition and subtraction.

Circle

The circumference of a circle is the outer edge and is calculated with the equation Pi × diameter. The area can be calculated with the equation Pi × the square of its radius.

A cord is any straight line drawn from one part of the circumference to another. A straight line taken from the circumference to the centre is called the radius; and a straight line from one part of the circumference to another, which passes through the centre, is called the diameter. When a circle has a cord drawn on it, the circle is divided into two segments.

Congruent

If shapes, for example squares or triangles, have the same angles and all the lengths are the same, they are said to be congruent. Shapes are said to be similar if the angles are the same and the ratio of all the corresponding lengths are equal.

Cube

A cube has six square faces at right angles to each other. The cube of a number is established if the number is multiplied by itself twice: for example, the cube of 5 = 5 × 5 × 5 (answer 125). We would say that the cube root of 125 is 5. The sign for cube root is $\sqrt[3]{}$.

Decimal number

A decimal number has a decimal point. The point serves to separate the whole number from the decimal fraction. Some decimals are recurring. Decimal places after the point represent, respectively, tenths, hundredths, thousandths and so on.

Distance

To work out distance multiply rate of travel by time.

Division

You do not often have to do long division in a selection test, especially if the sum is awkward. Some test publishers, however, want to establish if you are aware of the short cuts and useful features of mathematics. For this reason it is worth looking to see if the question has been formed so as to test whether you realise the following:

- A number is divisible by 2 if its last digit is even.
- A number is divisible by 5 if its last number is either 5 or 0.
- A number is divisible by 10 if its last number is 0 (remember that to divide by 10, simply take off the 0).
- A number is divisible by 3 if the sum of its digits is divisible by 3.
- A number is divisible by 9 if the sum of its digits is divisible by 9.
- A number is divisible by 4 if the number formed by the last two digits is divisible by 4.
- A number is divisible by 8 if the number formed by the last 3 digits is divisible by 8.
- A number is divisible by 6 if it is also divisible by both 2 and 3.

Equation

An equation involves an equal sign (=) and is used to express the fact that two quantities are equal.

The type of equations tested in graduate and manager selection tests are linear and quadratic equations. Quadratic equations involve variables with a power of 2. There are a number of methods which can be used to solve them and it is best to stick to the method with which you are already familiar. If you are unfamiliar with quadratic equations then seek further explanation before you attend for a test.

Exponent

An exponent is the power to which something has been raised. For example, the exponent is 2 in the term 10 to the power of 2 and this would be expressed as 10^2.

Factor

A factor is a whole number which will divide into another whole number exactly. The factors of, for example, 8 are 1, 2, 4 and 8.

Factorise

If you factorise an equation or mathematics expression you separate it into bracketed parts which, if multiplied together, will give that expression.

Fraction

A fraction is a part of a whole number. You need to be able to work with both decimal and vulgar fractions. Decimal fractions are described in the entry entitled 'decimal number'. Vulgar fractions use two whole numbers, one above the other. These are called the denominator (the lower number) and the numerator (the upper number). An improper fraction is one where the numerator is bigger than the denominator.

Fractions can be changed to another equivalent fraction and still have the same value. You should always finish a calculation by expressing a fraction in its lowest term.

To change a fraction to a lower equivalent you look to divide both the numerator and denominator by the same number. This is called cancelling. If the number is even you can always divide by 2. Sometimes you cancel more than once before you arrive at the lowest equivalent.

To add or subtract fractions you need to ensure that all the denominators are the same. In the example:

$$\frac{1}{2} + \frac{3}{8} = ?$$

Find the common denominator which is 8 and convert to eighths =

$$\frac{4}{8} + \frac{3}{8} \text{ . The answer is } \frac{7}{8}$$

To multiply fractions, make sure any mixed numbers (whole numbers and fractions) are converted into improper fractions and then multiply all the numerators and all the denominators together.

To divide fractions change any mixed numbers into improper fractions and then turn the fraction upside down (invert it) and multiply.

Frequency

Frequency is the number of times an event occurs.

Generalise

If we find a pattern and express it using algebraic expressions we are said to have generalised it.

Graph

A graph is a diagram comprising two reference lines, called axes, at right angles to each other. A scale is marked along each axis. Graphs are used to show a relationship between two quantities. Before you begin to calculate with figures taken from a graph, take care that the units are comparable and that you are looking in the correct column or line. See X and Y.

Histogram

A histogram is similar to a bar chart except that it is the areas of the bars which represent the frequency or quantity rather than the length of the bars.

Inequalities

These are signs used to indicate relative size. For example:

$$> \quad \text{means greater than}$$
$$< \quad \text{means less than}$$

Interest: compound and simple

You may well face questions which require you to work out simple or, more likely, compound interest.

Simple interest involves a quantity of money and a rate of interest. You simply multiply the amount of money by the rate of interest and divide by 100 to establish the interest earned.

Compound interest is the type most banks offer. The interest is added to the amount saved and you then receive interest on both the sum saved and the interest. You can save a great deal of time if you use a formula to calculate compound interest. To work out the total amount of compound interest earned, use the following formula:

$$\text{Final amount} = P \times (1 + \tfrac{R}{100})^N$$

Where: P = Amount initially invested
R = Percentage rate of interest
N = Number of years investment made

Mean, Median and Mode See Average.

Multiplication

Make sure the units of each number are underneath each other. To multiply any whole number by 10, 100, 1,000 and so on, simply add a 0 in the case of multiplying by 10, two 00s in the case of 100, etc.

To multiply decimals, ignore the decimal points and proceed as if the numbers were whole. When you have finished multiplying, count for each decimal how many figures (including 0s) there are to the right of the decimal point and add them together. The total gives you the number of decimal figures to the right of the point you must have in your answer. As you are not usually allowed a calculator, it may pay to revise the multiplication tables set out overleaf.

Percentage

Percentage is a way of describing parts of a whole. One per cent (1%) means one out of one hundred. To calculate, for example, 25% of 300 we calculate:

$$300 \times \frac{25}{100} = 75$$

Percentage as fractions. A percentage is a fraction with a denominator of 100. To express a percentage as a fraction, all you need to do is express it as its lowest term.

Percentage as decimals. To change a percentage into a decimal all you need to do is divide by 100. You can do this by moving the decimal point 2 places towards the left.

Changing fractions and decimals into percentages. Multiply by 100.

Percentage increase and decrease. To work out a percentage decrease or increase you compare the decrease or increase with the original amount.

If an amount is to be decreased by, for example, 20% then we need to calculate 100 − 20 = 80% of the total. Likewise, if we want to increase an amount by, say, 10% we have to calculate 110% of the original amount.

To work out 80% of £14 we use the following method:

$$80\% = \frac{(80)}{100} \times 14 = £11.20$$

1 × 2 = 2			1 × 3 = 3			1 × 4 = 4		
2 × 2 = 4			2 × 3 = 6			2 × 4 = 8		
3 × 2 = 6			3 × 3 = 9			3 × 4 = 12		
4 × 2 = 8			4 × 3 = 12			4 × 4 = 16		
5 × 2 = 10			5 × 3 = 15			5 × 4 = 20		
6 × 2 = 12			6 × 3 = 18			6 × 4 = 24		
7 × 2 = 14			7 × 3 = 21			7 × 4 = 28		
8 × 2 = 16			8 × 3 = 24			8 × 4 = 32		
9 × 2 = 18			9 × 3 = 27			9 × 4 = 36		
10 × 2 = 20			10 × 3 = 30			10 × 4 = 40		
11 × 2 = 22			11 × 3 = 33			11 × 4 = 44		
12 × 2 = 24			12 × 3 = 36			12 × 4 = 48		

1 × 5 = 5			1 × 6 = 6			1 × 7 = 7		
2 × 5 = 10			2 × 6 = 12			2 × 7 = 14		
3 × 5 = 15			3 × 6 = 18			3 × 7 = 21		
4 × 5 = 20			4 × 6 = 24			4 × 7 = 28		
5 × 5 = 25			5 × 6 = 30			5 × 7 = 35		
6 × 5 = 30			6 × 6 = 36			6 × 7 = 42		
7 × 5 = 35			7 × 6 = 42			7 × 7 = 49		
8 × 5 = 40			8 × 6 = 48			8 × 7 = 56		
9 × 5 = 45			9 × 6 = 54			9 × 7 = 63		
10 × 5 = 50			10 × 6 = 60			10 × 7 = 70		
11 × 5 = 55			11 × 6 = 66			11 × 7 = 77		
12 × 5 = 60			12 × 6 = 72			12 × 7 = 84		

1 × 8 = 8			1 × 9 = 9			1 × 10 = 10		
2 × 8 = 16			2 × 9 = 18			2 × 10 = 20		
3 × 8 = 24			3 × 9 = 27			3 × 10 = 30		
4 × 8 = 32			4 × 9 = 36			4 × 10 = 40		
5 × 8 = 40			5 × 9 = 45			5 × 10 = 50		
6 × 8 = 48			6 × 9 = 54			6 × 10 = 60		
7 × 8 = 56			7 × 9 = 63			7 × 10 = 70		
8 × 8 = 64			8 × 9 = 72			8 × 10 = 80		
9 × 8 = 72			9 × 9 = 81			9 × 10 = 90		
10 × 8 = 80			10 × 9 = 90			10 × 10 = 100		
11 × 8 = 88			11 × 9 = 99			11 × 10 = 110		
12 × 8 = 96			12 × 9 = 108			12 × 10 = 120		

Value added tax and profit and loss

Test questions of percentage are often concerned with value added tax (VAT) or profit and loss.

VAT

Ensure you are able to work out the amount of VAT to be charged and the amount of VAT contained within an inclusive sum. The first of these is easy. To work out the VAT included in a total use the following method:

Treat the inclusive sum as 100% + the percentage rate of VAT. Then work out 100% of the total.

Practice question

If a car costs £11,750 inclusive of VAT at 17.5%, how much was the car excluding VAT?

If you take the total price to equal 117.5% then you can work out the VAT paid and so the exclusive price of the car as follows:

$$\frac{11750}{117.5} \times 100 = 1000$$

Therefore the price of the car exclusive of VAT = £10,750.

Profit and loss

We buy goods at one price and sell them at another. Test questions often expect profit or loss to be expressed as a percentage. The way to approach these questions is as follows:

1. Work out the cash profit or loss
2. Express this as a fraction of the original (buying) price
3. Convert this fraction to a percentage

Practice question

A shop buys watches for £10 and sells them for £16. What is the percentage profit?

Answer = 60%

Pi

The sign for Pi is π and is found by dividing the circumference of a circle by its diameter.

Picograms

A picogram is a representation of information which uses pictures to denote the frequency or quantity.

Pie chart

A pie chart divides a circle into sectors, the size of which represents a portion of the whole.

Powers

See Exponent.

Priorities

See Brackets.

Probability

The likelihood of an event happening is expressed as a fraction. If something is impossible then the probability is 0, if there is an even chance it is expressed as $\frac{1}{2}$ and if an event is a certainty it is expressed as 1. The probability of a dice being rolled and it coming to rest with the number 3 at the top is $\frac{1}{6}$.

Quartiles

If you have a graph demonstrating the cumulative frequency of a quantity, it may be divided into equal quarters and these are called quartiles of a distribution. Quartiles are added to the graph by dividing the total frequency into equal groups. You have an upper and lower quartile and the median.

Ratio

Ratio is a comparison of quantities. Like fractions, they can be simplified or cancelled down. For example, if you are told that the ratio between men and women is 25:50 this can be simplified to 1:2.

Running totals or cumulative frequency

A running total allows you to realise the total to date and find out the median and the quartiles of distribution. If drawn on a graph, the cumulative frequency will form a distinctive curve known as the ogive.

Segment

See Circle.

Set

A set is a collection or class of items which have something in common. In mathematics a set is indicated by this type of bracket: { }. An example of a set (in this case a finite set) is the set of positive numbers under 10 = {1 2 3 4 5 6 7 8 9}.

Square root

The square root of a number is that number which, if multiplied by itself, would give you your original number. For example, the square root of 25 is 5 because $5 \times 5 = 25$. Every number has both a positive and a negative square root. The square roots of 25 are both 5 and –5 (remember, if two minus numbers are multiplied, they equal a positive).

Subtraction

There are two widely practised methods of subtraction. I will illustrate the point with the following example:

$$\begin{array}{r} 93 \\ -27 \\ \hline 66 \end{array}$$

In method A, you would borrow 10 from the 9 to make the 3 = 13, the 9 would then become an 8. In method B, we would again add 10 to the 3 to make it 13 but this time we would also add 10 to the 2 on the bottom line to make it 3.

Stick with whichever method you were taught.

Triangle

The sum of the inside angles of a triangle is always 180 degrees. An equilateral triangle is one with three equal sides, and three equal angles, all, therefore, of 60 degrees. A right-angled triangle is one with a right angle. An isosceles triangle is one with two equal sides and two equal angles.

Volume

Volume is the measurement of the three-dimensional space occupied by a solid. It is quantifiable in cubic measurement, for example, cubic metres.

There are formulae for finding volume in all the regular shapes. To find the volume of a box, for instance, you multiply length by breadth by height. To find the volume of shapes which have vertical sides of equal length, for example a cylinder or a triangular prism, you multiply the area of the base by the height.

Whole numbers

Examples of whole numbers are 0, 1, 2, 3, 4 and so on. A whole number which is divisible by 2 is called an even number. A number not divisible by 2 is an odd number. Note that a number is said to be divisible only if a second number divides into it without any remainder.

X and Y

The horizontal (X) and vertical (Y) axes on a two-dimensional graph are referred to as the X and Y axes.

Part 3
Practice questions

1. A till role is 10 metres long while the average till receipt is 8cm long. How many customers can be served before the till roll needs to be changed?

    Answer

2. A store serves 6000 customers a day. Given that the average till receipt is 8cm long and a till roll is 10 metres long, how many till roles will be used each day?

    Answer

3. A household's water bill was £240 and is charged at 15 pence a gallon. How many gallons of water did the household use?

    Answer

4. A household's water bill of £240 is to increase by 12%. What will be the new total?

    Answer

5. If a water bill of £240 includes VAT at 17.5%, how much VAT will be paid? Express your answer to the nearest whole penny.

Answer

6. The pages in a novel have on average 50 lines comprising 12 words. If in total there are 175 pages, how many words does the novel contain?

Answer

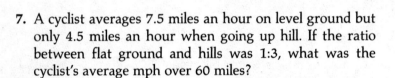

7. A cyclist averages 7.5 miles an hour on level ground but only 4.5 miles an hour when going up hill. If the ratio between flat ground and hills was 1:3, what was the cyclist's average mph over 60 miles?

Answer

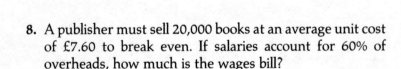

8. A publisher must sell 20,000 books at an average unit cost of £7.60 to break even. If salaries account for 60% of overheads, how much is the wages bill?

Answer

9. A box of chocolates comprises 12 chocolates and weighs ¾ of a pound. If the packaging weighs ⅕ of the total, how much does each chocolate weigh? Express your answer as a fraction of a pound.

Answer

10. A garage discovered that ½ of their customers bought French cars, ⅓ German cars and ⅙ (20) American. How many customers did the garage have?

Answer

11. How much is ⅗ of £750?

Answer

12. One-half of the turnover of a business is spent on salaries, one-third on production and distribution. After setting aside £10,000 for marketing, there is £23,000 left. How much is the total turnover?

Answer

13. In a sale goods were advertised at ¼ of their marked price. What was the total sale price for:

A calculator marked price	£5.90
A book marked price	£17.30
Jeans marked price	£44.00

Answer

14. To travel to work a woman spends 70 pence on bus fare and 120 pence on train fare. She spends the same amount on the way home. In a normal working week how much would she save if she bought a travel pass at £14.50?

Answer

15. A man purchased a lottery ticket each week (52 weeks a year) for six years. He worked out that he would have to win £624 to recoup his money. How much did each ticket cost?

Answer

16. A full price return ticket to Liverpool costs £84. If you travel after 9.30 am the cost drops to £32. What percentage saving does this represent?

Answer

17. There are only 24 women out of a total workforce of 1200 in an engineering company. What is the ratio of female to male employees?

Answer

18. Beer is sold at 190 pence a pint at a bar which sells 2 barrels, each containing 30 gallons, a week. How much income does the bar gain from beer each week? (Note that a gallon comprises 8 pints.)

Answer

19. Find the compound interest on £2000 invested for 3 years at 5% per annum (pa).

Answer

20. A 16kg sack of potatoes costs £4.50. How much does a kilogram of potatoes cost? Express your answer to the nearest whole penny.

Answer

21. A bank offers 6% pa interest calculated annually. Another offers 5% interest calculated every six months. What is the difference paid at the end of the year on a deposit of £1000?

Answer

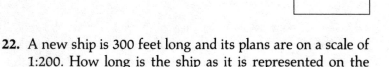

22. A new ship is 300 feet long and its plans are on a scale of 1:200. How long is the ship as it is represented on the plans?

Answer

23. An investment of £10,000 earns interest at 6% pa fixed for a 5-year period. How much will the total investment with interest amount to at the end of the 5-year period?

Answer

24. A business loan of £2000 is to have interest charged at 20% pa. How much will the monthly repayments be if both the interest and loan are to be repaid in one year?

Answer

25. The interest on a car loan of £3000 is to be charged at 15% pa. How much will the monthly repayments be if both the loan and interest are to be repaid in 24 months? Express your answer to the nearest penny.

Answer

26. A box of 100 pens is bought for £5 and sold for 8 pence each. What is the percentage profit?

Answer

27. A table was sold for £280 at a 20% loss. What was the buying price?

Answer

28. A watch cost £9 + VAT which is charged at 17.5%. What is the total price to be paid?

Answer

29. An estimate is made for £2000 + VAT (at 17.5%) for the preparation of a business plan. How much VAT is to be paid?

Answer

30. A restaurant bill totals £110.00 inclusive of VAT and a service charge. VAT was charged at 17.5% after a service charge of 10% was levied. How much was the bill excluding the VAT and service charge? Express your answer to the nearest penny.

Answer

31. A photocopier service contract costs £40 a month excluding VAT (at 17.5%). How much VAT is paid in 12 months?

Answer

32. A cooker is sold for £800 inclusive of VAT which is charged at 17.5%. How much did the cooker cost excluding VAT?

Answer

33. Divide £50 into the ratio of 3:2.

Answer

34. Components A, B and C are ordered in the ratio of 1:5:4. How many of each are included in an order which totals 1000 components?

Answer

35. In some cities in the United Kingdom male unemployment is as high as 30% of the total economically active population. Express this level of unemployment as a ratio.

Answer

36. On a housing estate 60% of the unemployed were found to have last worked in the construction industry, while 24% last worked in the public service sector; and 16% were found to have last worked in retail and distribution. Express these quantities as a ratio.

Answer

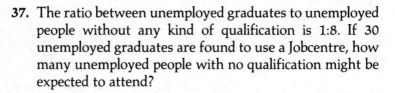

37. The ratio between unemployed graduates to unemployed people without any kind of qualification is 1:8. If 30 unemployed graduates are found to use a Jobcentre, how many unemployed people with no qualification might be expected to attend?

Answer

38. A woman earns £13,000 and has a single person's allowance of £2800. How much tax would she pay? Assume the rate of tax is 24%.

Answer

39. A man earns £200 a week. He pays tax at 24% on all earnings over his annual allowance of £2300. How much tax does he pay each week? Express your answer to the nearest penny.

Answer

40. If tax is charged at 24%, how much is payable on a taxable income of £10,000?

Answer

41. A car travels 70 miles in 2 and a half hours. What is its average speed?

Answer

42. A train travels at an average speed of 110 mph. How long does it take to travel 385 miles?

Answer

43. A yacht averages 4 nautical miles an hour but the tide is running against it at one knot an hour. How long will the yacht take to reach a harbour 1.5 nautical miles away? (Note that 1 knot an hour = 1 nautical mile.)

Answer

44. The initial price of a computer is £99 but it was reduced in a sale by 10%. After a week a further 10% discount was made on the new price. What was the eventual asking price?

Answer

45. A machine produces 130 nuts in 10 minutes. A second machine produces 264 nuts in 12 minutes. How long would it take the two machines running simultaneously to produce 700 nuts?

Answer

46. A total of 5000 copies of a book were sold: 60% were sold at 50% discount, 20% were sold at 30% discount while the remainder were sold at the cover price of £6.99. What was the total revenue?

Answer

47. In an election the Yellow Party candidate received ½ as many votes as the Red Party candidate. The Red Party candidate received ⅓ more votes than the candidate from the Blue Party. In total 10,000 people voted for the Blue Party candidate. How many votes did the Yellow candidate receive?

Answer

48. In a sample of 220, 5% were positive. In a second sample of 120, 10% were positive. What was the combined percentage of positive responses?

Answer

49. A daisy wheel printer prints 20 characters a second and is four times faster than the average printer. If the average printer is 5 times faster than an electric typewriter, how many characters can an electric typewriter print?

Answer

50. After paying 24% tax on all income over £2300, a person has a net income of £12,000. What was the income before tax?

Answer

Answers to Chapter 3

Part 1
A diagnostic exercise (page 26)

1. 80,000	10. 37	19. 7:2
2. 391 miles	11. 235	20. 500
3. £123.30	12. 10 pence	21. 60cl
4. 2925	13. $1\frac{5}{36}$	22. 12.25
5. 49,699	14. $1\frac{7}{8}$	23. £14.25
6. 43 units	15. 1610	24. 84
7. 2380	16. 0.0625	25. £2.15
8. £16.48	17. 17.871	26. £27.75
9. 3600	18. 2174	27. £4255.32

Part 3
Practice questions (page 47)

1. 125	19. £315.25	35. 3:10
2. 48	20. 28 pence	36. 15:6:4
3. 1600 gallons	21. £42.50	37. 240
4. £268.80	22. 18 inches	38. £2448
5. £35.74	23. £13,382.26	39. £37.38
6. 105,000	24. £200	40. £2400
7. 5 mph	25. £165.31	41. 28 mph
8. £91,200	26. 60%	42. $3\frac{1}{2}$ hours
9. $\frac{1}{20}$ pound	27. £350	43. 30 minutes
10. 120	28. £10.58	44. £80.19
11. £450	29. £350	45. 20 minutes
12. £198,000	30. £85.11	46. £22,368
13. £16.80	31. £84	47. 6667 votes
14. £4.50	32. £680.85	48. 23
15. £2	33. £30:£20	
16. 62%	34. A = 100	
17. 1:49	B = 500	
18. £912	C = 400	

Chapter 4

Relearn the Rules of English Usage

To write or speak English, or, for that matter, any natural language, involves rules of usage, called grammar.

To speak or write correctly you do not need to be able to recite these rules of usage. The grammar classes at school can be a distant, possibly bad, memory and the content of those lessons long forgotten. In order to speak or write correctly, it is required only that you apply the rules correctly, that you implicitly follow the rules.

In the context of a selection test, however, the correct application of the rules is insufficient. To do well in such tests it is necessary that you know, as well as follow, the rules of usage. For most, this requires a certain amount of revision. It is well worth the effort. The test candidate who knows the rules will be far more confident, will realise what is behind the examiner's questions and will recognise the significance of the subtle differences in the suggested answers.

What follows is a statement of the rules of written and spoken English. I have tried to make the entries brief and clear reviews of the elements of grammar relevant to tests. The practice questions which follow the glossary allow you to practise the rules.

Practice questions (page 60)

49. 1
50. £14,328

Part 1
Glossary

Adjective

An adjective adds detail to a noun or pronoun. To say, for example, that the record was scratched is to add the adjective 'scratched' to the noun 'record'.

Adjectives can also limit or define. For this reason it is proper to think of them as modifiers. For example, if we say that 'Few people enjoy the game', the adjective 'few' limits rather than describes the noun 'people'.

Adverb

An adverb modifies a verb. It can detail, limit or define. If we say, for example, 'The yacht was sinking fast', the adverb 'fast' adds detail to the verb 'sinking'. 'Not' and 'very' are adverbs. An adverb can also add detail to an adjective (very few) or another adverb (very fast).

Note that adjectives and adverbs can be either phrases or words. In the statement 'The people opposite me enjoyed the game', the phrase 'opposite me' limits the noun 'people', so is an adjective.

Apposition

An appositional word or phrase is a noun or pronoun placed next to another noun or pronoun. It has the same meaning but its function is to rename or identify the subject. For example, if I were to say, 'The child, Junior, drank all the milk', I would be introducing a one-word apposition: 'Junior'. An example of an appositional phrase is 'a one-year-old' in the statement 'The child, a one-year-old, drank all the milk'.

Article

Articles modify nouns. They are either indefinite or definite. 'A' and 'an' are indefinite articles because they modify a singular noun which is general. The article 'the' is particular so is used to modify a particular noun.

Clause

A clause is a group of words within a sentence which contains a subject and a verb. If you were to say, for example, 'They bought the camera in order to photograph the baby', you have two clauses: first clause, 'They bought the camera' (subject 'camera', verb 'bought'); second clause, 'in order to photograph the baby' (subject 'baby', verb 'photograph').

There are two types of clause:

Main clause
A main clause expresses a complete thought and makes sense on its own. The example 'They bought the camera' is a main clause.

Subordinate clause
A subordinate clause on its own does not make sense or express a complete thought. 'In order to photograph the baby' is an example of a subordinate clause.

Complement

The basic parts of a sentence are a subject, a verb and a complement. The complement follows the subject and verb to complete the meaning. It can be any word or phrase. For example:

'Scott went on holiday.' (The complement is the noun 'holiday', 'Scott' the subject and 'went' the verb.)

'Describe the taste to me.' (The complement is the pronoun 'me', 'taste' the subject, 'describe' the verb.)

Conjunction

A conjunction is a word which joins words, phrases or clauses. A conjunction can either treat clauses equally or make one more important. A co-ordinating conjunction connects without making either part more important and usually involves a comma being placed before the conjunction. Examples are 'or', 'for', 'so', 'but' and 'nor'. A subordinating conjunction makes the clause it begins less important. Examples are 'as', 'because', 'when' and 'which'.

Direct object

A direct object is a complement to which the verb in a sentence is directed. It is either a noun or pronoun, phrase or clause. In the examples provided in the entry for Complement, both the words 'holiday' and 'me' are direct objects of the verbs 'went' and 'describe' respectively.

Gerund

A gerund is used as a noun but is formed from a verb (so it is a verbal; see page 72). It ends in '-ing' and often begins a phrase. For example:

'Playing all day was exhausting.' (The gerund is 'playing', formed from the verb 'to play', but used in this context as a noun.)

'Smoking causes cancer.'

'She loves cycling in the open countryside.' (In this instance, the gerund is not at the beginning of the sentence.)

Indirect object

A sentence which contains an indirect object must also contain a direct object because the former indicates to whom or what the action of the verb is directed. Like a direct object, an indirect object is a complement. For example, take the sentence: 'Thomas wanted the videos for his students.' In this case the subject is 'Thomas', the verb 'wanted', the direct object 'the videos' and 'his students' the indirect object.

Infinitive

An infinitive consists of the word 'to' followed by a verb used as either a noun, an adjective or an adverb. For example:

'To smile is bliss.' (The verb 'to smile' is here being used as a noun.)

'If only you were to smile.' (The verb 'to smile' is here being used as an adjective.)

'She tried hard to smile.' (The verb 'to smile' is here being used as an adverb.)

Watch out for split infinitives. A split infinitive has an adverb placed between the 'to' and the verb. A famous example is 'to boldly go'. To avoid splitting the infinitive the phrase should read 'to go boldly'.

Interjection

An interjection is a word which expresses an emotion and is not grammatically related to the sentence in which it is found. If you say, for example, 'Yes, we won the contract.' In this case, the word 'yes' constitutes an interjection.

Modifier

A modifier adds information and may take the form of a word, a phrase or a clause. Adjectives, adverbs and articles are examples of modifiers.

Misplaced modifier
A modifier is misplaced if, in a sentence, it modifies the wrong word; if it seems to describe a thing or person other than the thing or person it should describe. To correct the situation, you simply move the modifier. For example:

'The reporter went to the press briefing to hear about the escaped lion with a tape recorder.'

This should have read:

'The reporter with the tape recorder went to the press briefing to hear about the escaped lion.'

Dangling modifier

A modifier is said to dangle if it cannot be attached to the subject of the main clause so, unless the sentence is changed, it has nothing to modify. For example:

'Before writing a press release, the reader should be considered.'

The phrase 'Before writing a press release' is a dangling modifier because it does not have a subject to modify. To correct the situation the sentence would need to be changed so that it read, for example:

'Before writing a press release, the writer should consider the reader.'

Noun

A noun is a word, a clause or a phrase which identifies a person, a place, an idea or a thing. There are five types of noun:

Proper noun

A proper noun names a particular person, place or thing. Examples of proper nouns are 'Tony', 'France' and 'Taj Mahal'. Note that proper nouns always begin with a capital letter.

Common noun

A common noun identifies a general thing, a place or a kind of person. For example: 'house', 'village green' or 'traffic warden'.

Collective noun

Collective nouns are singular but they identify groups of individuals. For example: 'audience', 'class' and 'crowd'.

Concrete noun

Concrete nouns identify inanimate objects such as 'mineral', 'metal', 'paper' and 'feather'. Common nouns can also be concrete nouns; for example, 'chair' and 'table' are both common and concrete nouns.

Abstract noun

Abstract nouns identify qualities and ideals such as 'truth', 'justice' and 'intelligence'.

Participle

A participle is formed from a verb which is used like an adjective. A present participle ends in '-ing' while a past participle usually ends in '-ed', '-en' or '-t'. An example of a present participle is 'paying' in the sentence: 'Paying tax is a necessary evil.' An example of a past participle is 'celebrated' in the sentence: 'The celebrated climber gave a speech.'

Watch out for dangling participial phrases. A participial phrase begins with a participle. It is dangling if there is no noun or pronoun to which it adds detail. For example, the following statement contains a dangling participial phrase:

'Having finished the crossword, the dog went out into the garden.'

The participial phrase 'Having finished the crossword' is dangling because there is no sensible noun or pronoun to which it relates. To make the statement sensible, you would need to provide a noun or pronoun. For example:

'Having finished the crossword, Thomas went out into the garden with the dog.'

Parts of speech

There are eight basic types of word: nouns, pronouns, verbs, adjectives, adverbs, prepositions, conjunctions and interjectives.

Pronoun

A pronoun can be used in place of a noun. For example:

'The water was warm, and it remained so all day.'

The pronoun 'it' has been used in this sentence in place of the noun 'water'.

When replacing nouns with pronouns, you need to take care that you do not introduce ambiguity. For example: 'The water remained warm all day, and it was the warmest I can remember.' In this instance it is unclear whether it is the water or the day which was the warmest in memory. When there is a risk of ambiguity the noun should be repeated. For example, in the above case the ambiguity is removed if we write: 'The water remained warm all day, the warmest day I can remember.'

There are a great many pronouns and they are classified by function. The list here is not exhaustive:

Demonstrative pronouns:	This, that, these, those.
Interrogative pronouns:	Which?, who?, whom?, what?, whose?
Personal pronouns:	I, he, you, she, us, them.
Possessive pronouns:	My, mine, your, its, his, her, our, their.
Indefinite pronouns:	All, both, few, many, some.

Sentence

A sentence must have a subject and a verb and express a complete thought. For example, the statement, 'Opera began' has a subject (Opera) and a verb (began) but does not express a complete thought, so is not a sentence. The situation is easily corrected if we write, 'The Opera began', as this does express a complete thought and so is a sentence. 'They cried' is an example of a sentence which comprises no more than a subject and a verb yet still expresses a complete thought.

Sentences are classified according to what they express or by their structure. In the context of selection tests, their classification according to structure is more relevant.

Sentences can be classified under four types of structure. These are:

1. Simple sentences
A simple sentence comprises one main clause only. So remember that a main clause can be a sentence. Examples are

69

usually short, for instance, 'She hates grammar'; but they need not be, as the following example illustrates:

'The assistant editor made over twenty suggested alterations in the first few pages of text.'

2. *Compound sentences*
A compound sentence has a multiple of main clauses (two or more). For example:

1st main clause	'Come and see our range of mountain bikes
Connective	and
2nd main clause	we will be pleased to demonstrate any model.'

3. *Complex sentences*
A complex sentence comprises one main clause and one or more subordinate clauses. For example:

Subordinate clause	After having a bath
Main clause	Thomas felt a lot better.

4. *Compound-complex sentences*
These comprise two or more main clauses and one or more subordinate clauses. For example:

1st main clause	Thomas so enjoyed the opera,
1st subordinate clause	which he had heard was good,
2nd main clause	that he vowed to go each week
2nd subordinate clause	assuming he could obtain tickets.

In English usage tests look out for two or more sentences which are joined by a comma or have no punctuation separating them. For example: 'The sun shone, they were very happy.' This kind of error is often examined and can be corrected with either a full stop, a semicolon or the use of the conjunction 'and' in place of the comma.

Another common error examined in selection tests involves a phrase or subordinate clause being presented as a sentence.

Subject

A subject is the word or words being talked about in the sentence. A subject is often a noun but can be a pronoun, a verbal noun (but not a participle), a phrase or a clause. A subject has one or more verbs which tell what the subject is doing.

The subject is underlined in the following sentences:

'Oystercatchers are black and white wading birds.'
(Subject as a noun)

'After showering, she went to work.'
(Subject as a pronoun)

'Rain making is impossible.'
(Subject as a gerund phrase)

'What is happening is quite the most extraordinary thing imaginable.'
(Subject as a subordinate clause)

Tense

Tense shows the moment to which a verb refers. A simple tense can show the past, present or future. For example: he swam, he swims, he will swim. What are called perfect tenses can be further subdivided (notice that all three contain past participles):

1. *Present perfect tense.* This shows that an action which began in the past is continuing or has been completed in the present. For example: 'Birthdays are always celebrated.'
2. *Past perfect (or pluperfect) tense.* This shows that an action was completed before a past point in time. For example: 'Gino had finished his birthday celebration by midnight.'

71

3. *Future perfect tense.* This shows that a future action will be completed after another future action. For example: 'By the time this book is published, my first child will have been born.'

In a verbal usage exam always check that the tenses of a sentence are not mixed up. In particular, ensure that the verb in the subordinate clause has the same tense as the verb in the main clause.

Verb

A verb tells what someone, or something, is or does, its state or condition. There are two types of action verb – transitive and intransitive. 'She <u>publishes</u> books': 'publishes' is a transitive verb because it is followed by a direct object. In the sentence, 'The river <u>winds</u> through the hills', 'winds' is an intransitive verb as it is not followed by a direct object. There are also linking verbs; for example, 'The sea <u>looks</u> green' and 'she <u>is</u> accomplished' – these tell us what someone or something is.

Questions in selection tests are sometimes based on the characteristics of verbs, in particular, the number, person and tense of a verb.

1. Number
A verb must agree with the number of its subject. If, for example, the subject is plural so must the verb be. Consider an example – 'Mother and baby does well' is incorrect because the subject is plural while the verb is singular.

2. Person
A verb can be in the first, second or third person (singular or plural) and serves to establish whether or not the subject is speaking, being addressed or being spoken about. The same verb form often applies to different persons and numbers:

'We <u>won</u> the race.' (plural first person)

'You <u>won</u> the race.' (singular or plural second person)
'They <u>won</u> the race.' (plural third person)

3. Tense
Tense shows whether or not the verb refers to the past, present or future. The verb of any subordinate clause must agree with the tense of the main clause. For example, the sentence, 'After he read the paper, Jon asks anyone else if they would like to read it', is incorrect because the verb in the main clause is in the present tense while the verb in the subordinate clause is in the past tense.

Verbal

A verbal is derived from a verb but is not used as such. Verbals are, instead, used as either nouns, adjectives or infinitives. See Gerund, Participle and Infinitive for examples.

Part 2
Practice questions

Identify the correct sentences:

1.

A There are redundancies when the managing director arrived.
B There will be redundancies after the managing director arrived.
C After the new managing director arrived, there were redundancies.
D After the new managing director arrived, there will be many redundancies.
E None of these.

Answer

2.

A As soon as the sales figures are available, the directors knew they had achieved their targets.
B As soon as the sales figures were available, the directors knew they had achieved their targets.
C As soon as the sales figures are available, the directors knew they have achieved their targets.
D None of these.

Answer

3.

A Although the business plan look promising the bank manager suspected that the proposal is unlikely to succeed.

B Although the business plan looks promising the bank manager suspects that the proposal was unlikely to succeed.

C Although the business plan looked promising the bank manager suspected that the proposal was unlikely to succeed.

D None of these.

Answer

4.

A If you were to contact the client you might find that they would buy.

B If you are to contact the client you might find that they would buy.

C If you were to contact the client you will find that they will buy.

D None of these.

Answer

5.

A While the photocopier is broken you will have to go across the road to the copy shop.

B While the photocopier was broken you will have to go across the road to the copy shop.

C When the photocopier is broken you went across the road to the copy shop.

D None of these.

Answer

6.

A My new colleague is the one who has the red car.

B My new colleague was the one whom had the red car.

C My new colleague will be the one who had the red car.

D None of these.

Answer

7.

A The family will eating their meal in the restaurant.

B The family was eating its meal in the restaurant.

C The family were eating their meal in the restaurant.

D None of these.

Answer

8.

A Neither you nor I is able to make sense of this.
B Neither you nor I are able to make sense of this.
C Neither you or I will be able to make sense of this.
D None of these.

Answer

9.

A Bill, as well as the rest of his colleagues, is going to the annual office dinner.
B Bill, as well as the rest of his colleagues, are going to the annual office dinner.
C Neither of these.

Answer

10.

A You girls over there what do you think you are doing.
B You girl over there what do you think you are doing.
C Neither of these.

Answer

Identify any *incorrect* sentences. The error for which you are looking is a dangling participial phrase.

11.

A Having read of the outbreak of unrest in Africa, Joe heard the next day that war had broken out.
B The Prime Minister decided to recall Parliament; he faced a sea of very grave faces when he rose to make his statement.
C Having read of the outbreak of unrest in Africa, the next day war broke out.
D None of these.

Answer

12.

A Wishing the department to succeed, new staff were taken on.
B It was clear that the Prime Minister had written off the by-election result; he intended to blame it on the recession.
C Neither of these.

Answer

13.

A After having finished the exam, the candidates felt a great sense of relief.
B Feeling tired after the run, Hope decided to take a bath.
C My mother accused me of being mad, talking to myself all the time.
D None of these.

Answer

14.

A The mosquitoes drove him mad, walking through the jungle.
B When we got to the house, having walked for many hours, we simply fell into bed and slept.
C None of these.

Answer

15.

A Tests play an important role in the allocation of opportunities; their use, therefore, should be closely controlled.
B Woken from sleep by the bright sunshine, Mary decided to get up straightaway.
C Beaten roundly in battle by the French army, the English decided to sue for peace.
D None of these.

Answer

Split infinitives – identify the incorrect sentence:

16.

A From the age of three it was clear that Alison was going to quickly go to the top of the class.
B From the age of three it was clear that Alison was going to go quickly to the top of the class.
C Neither of these.

Answer

17.

A After going on her training course Susan was skilful in the way she managed to co-ordinate the concurrent sales and marketing conferences.
B After going on her training course Susan was able to co-ordinate skilfully the concurrent sales and marketing conferences.
C Neither of these.

Answer

18.

A It was clear that to precipitately press ahead would have been a mistake.

B It was clear that to press ahead precipitately would have been a mistake.

C Neither of these.

Answer

19.

A He wanted, at an accelerated pace, to move ahead, but his boss had prevented him from doing so.

B He wanted to move ahead at an accelerated pace, but his boss prevented him from doing so.

C Neither of these.

Answer

20.

A The sales team wished to really work hard in order to achieve their targets.

B The sales team wished really to work hard in order to achieve their targets.

C Neither of these.

Answer

21.

A Hoping to make amends, therefore, the Prime Minister called a special meeting of her cabinet.

B Hoping to, therefore, make amends the Prime Minister called a special meeting of his cabinet.

C Neither of these.

Answer

The following sentences test your understanding of the use of *apostrophes*. Identify the correct sentences. Note that more than one sentence may be correct.

22.

A It's a good thing you gave the baby lamb it's extra milk during the night.

B It's a good thing you gave the baby lamb its extra milk during the night.

C It is a good thing you gave the baby lamb its extra milk during the night.

D None of these.

Answer

23.

A Put the boys' shoes on otherwise their feet will get wet.
B Put the boy's shoes on otherwise their feet will get wet.
C Put the boys' shoes on otherwise his feet will get wet.
D None of these.

Answer

Useful tip: 'Its' (when used as a possessive) is an exception to the rule and does not take an apostrophe. Remember that the abbreviated form of 'it is' or 'it has' is 'it's', *with* an apostrophe.

24.

A Miles' achievement at cricket will long be remembered at his old school.
B Miles' achievements at cricket will long be remembered at his old school.
C Mile's achievement at cricket will long be remembered at his old school.
D None of these.

Answer

25.

A The 60s were a time when sexual liberation was first condoned.

B The 60's were a time when sexual liberation was first condoned.

C The sixty's were a time when sexual liberation was condoned.

D None of these.

Answer

26.

A The forecast for todays weather predicts rain, but tomorrow it's going to be fine.

B The forecast for today's weather predicts rain, but tomorrow its going to be fine.

C The forecast for todays weather predicts rain, but tomorrow its going to be fine.

D None of these.

Answer

Some tests require you to decide between parts of a sentence and identify which is correct.

With the following examples, your task is to identify which of the suggested parts complete the sentence correctly.

27.

Central banks had to step in to prop up the European Exchange Rate Mechanism . . .

A tomorrow if massive selling is not to threaten the French franc.

B yesterday as massive selling threatened the French franc.

C None of these.

Answer

28.

. . . cash offer under its recently announced enhanced dividend plan have come off best.

A The share-holders who subscribed to the companys

B The shareholder who sub-scribed for the company's

C The shareholder who subscribed to the company's

D None of these.

Answer

29.

Receivers were called in but they will attempt to keep the company trading, . . .

A it all depends on whether there are sufficient funds to pay salaries due on the last day of the month.
B and decide whether the company has sufficient funds to pay the salaries due on the last day of the month.
C if there are sufficient funds to pay this month's salaries.
D None of these.

Answer

30.

. . . they were frequently amended to allow for individual projects to be approved.

A Policy guidelines, agreed by the committee, however,
B Policy guidelines were agreed by the committee,
C Policy guidelines were agreed by the committee; however,
D None of these.

Answer

31.

. . . from the opposition when he called on them to change their minds and vote with the Government.

A He elicited a baying increase of support
B He elated a tremendous increase in support
C He elicited a baying crescendo of support
D None of these.

Answer

Use of *negatives*

32.

Only one of the following sentences is incorrect; which one is it?

A 'You don't want not to do that, do you?'
B 'I should not bother washing the car, dear,' said a wife to her husband, to which he replied, 'I can't not do it; it looks disgraceful.'
C He was stopped by the beggar, but hadn't got any money.
D You should not think there are no examples when killing could be warranted.
E It's not impossible that we will be able to get away tonight before 7 o'clock.

Answer

Use of *capitals*

33.

The capitalisation of three of the following sentences is incorrect. Which sentences are they?

A A person who comes from France will usually speak French.
B It was William Shakespeare who first coined the phrase 'all the world's a stage'.
C The Government buildings have all been renovated.
D After the management buy-out, Nicholas Smith took over as the new Managing Director.
E When asked which book he would take on his desert island, he said *'The Catcher in the Rye'*.
F Every morning we had to swear allegiance to the american flag.
G The Church situated on the corner is called The Church of St John.
H Sitting in the conference room were a group of managers, directors and other senior executives.

Answer

34.

Which of the following include incomplete sentences or do not form complete sentences?

A   He bought the Australian newspaper group. In order to complete his domination of the world's press.
B   To err is human.
C   'Passing my driving test is my greatest achievement so far'. She said.
D   The exhausted cyclist.
E   She got tanned. And the sun shone at the weekend.
F   Somewhere over the rainbow.
G   Having worked, she now decided to retire.

Answer

Practice punctuation

Which of the following sentences are correctly punctuated?

35.

A   For the sales conference, Alison had to check the seating, the lighting, the pen situation and the catering.
B   For the sales conference, Alison had to check the seating, the lighting, the pen situation, and the catering.
C   Neither sentence.

Answer

36.

A There were four boys chosen for the job; Toby, Scott, Miles and Mark.

B There were four boys chosen for the job: Toby, Scott, Miles and Mark.

C Neither sentence.

Answer

37.

A Although he could not be sure of his map reading, he decided to turn left at the next junction.

B Although he could not be sure of his map reading he decided to turn left at the next junction.

C Neither sentence.

Answer

38.

A Yes – he interjected, for he had to say exactly what he felt.

B Yes; he interjected, for he had to say exactly what he felt.

C Neither sentence.

Answer

39.

A Max, Bill and Geoff were in the room. So which boy's hat is this?

B Max, Bill and Geoff were in the room. So which boys' hat is this?

C Neither sentence.

Answer

40.

A The M25 is to be made into a 16-lane highway, many local residents find this unacceptable.

B The M25 is to be made into a 16-lane highway; many local residents find this unacceptable.

C Neither sentence.

Answer

41.

A He decided to become a full time student.

B He decided to become a full-time student.

C Neither sentence.

Answer

42.

A Would they need to ask the permission of the farmer to cross his land? it wasn't quite clear from the notice.

B Would they need to ask the permission of the farmer to cross his land; it wasn't quite clear from the notice?

C Neither sentence.

Answer

43.

A The MP, Crispin Biggs-Williams, was the first to declare his anti European intentions by waving his jacket – a brightly striped old Wellingtonian blazer – and was first into the opposition lobby.

B The MP Crispin Biggs-Williams, was the first to declare his anti European intentions by waving his jacket – a brightly striped old Wellingtonian blazer – and was first into the opposition lobby.

C Neither sentence.

Answer

44.

A "I am enjoying this" – he said, dreamily.

B 'I am enjoying this' – he said, dreamily.

C Neither sentence.

Answer

> Useful tips:
>
> When itemising a list do not include a comma before the final 'and' unless there has already been an 'and' in the list and a comma is needed for clarity. For example, had question 35 above read: 'For the sales conference, Alison had to check the seating, the lighting, the pen and paper situation, and the catering' then a comma before the final 'and' would be correct.
>
> The nouns which are linked together to describe another noun and precede it usually take a hyphen. For example, 'air-raid warden'.
>
> Remember – question marks and exclamation marks incorporate full stops and can, therefore, conclude a sentence.

Common spelling mistakes

45.

Underline the incorrect spellings below:

1. accomodation
2. miniscule
3. the affect
4. targetted
5. the business practice
6. fulfill
7. the current climate
8. the stationery car
9. the principle's office
10. indispensable
11. despairately
12. seperately
13. the mother's dependants
14. abysmaly
15. independant
16. shelfs
17. shere
18. sieve
19. bourgeoisy
20. necessarily
21. disatisfaction
22. trully
23. remittance
24. nascent
25. reminisence
26. conscientous
27. nationaly
28. potatoe
29. liklihood
30. psycopath
31. surreptitiously
32. participal
33. address
34. yatch
35. rooves
36. noticable
37. unnoticed
38. disoluble

39. realise
40. anti-clockwise
41. proceed
42. preceed
43. munifiscent
44. personel

45. persistant
46. perpetrator
47. jewellery
48. encyclopedia
49. inquiry
50. benefiting

Useful tips:

In most cases the 't's, 'l's and 'r's in the middle of a word are doubled; for example, pitting, fuelling and recurring. However, at the end of a word there is only one 't', 'l' or 'r'; for example, 'spiteful'. There are exceptions and you should learn the most common of these; examples include fulfil, benefited and targeted.

In most cases the prefixes 'dis', 'un', 'in', etc, take only one 's' or 'n' when attached to another word. However, remember that if the suffix already begins with an 's' or 'n', the letters will be doubled; for example, dissatisfaction and unnatural.

46.

Underline the correct choice in the following sentences:

A He was most complementary / complimentary about my new painting.

B The effect / affect you had on the children was to excite them.

C The tolling of the church bells, striking on the hour, every hour, was continuous / continual.

D Before disciplinary action is taken, advice / advise should be offered to the member of staff.

E By the time the starting pistol was fired, the runners were all ready / already for the race.

F The birthday cake was divided among / between the many guests.

G Children, put your toys back $^{into}_{in\ to}$ the toy box.

H You will find them $^{either}_{[no\ word\ is\ required]}$ in the wardrobe, on the chair or in the chest-of-drawers.

I After her engagement, she could not help but $^{flout}_{flaunt}$ her diamond ring at every opportunity.

J For my holiday in Africa, I was reminded to $^{take}_{bring}$ my malaria tablets.

K That case is quite different $^{from}_{than}$ the previous one we discussed.

L Booking is not required for families with $^{fewer}_{less}$ than five members.

M The pub is about half a mile $^{farther}_{further}$ down the road.

N We will be delighted if Tony and $^{you}_{yourself}$ join us for lunch.

O He had been $^{laying}_{lying}$ down for many hours before he was able to shake off his headache.

Mock test

Over the page you will find 25 questions. Do not turn the page until you are ready to begin. Allow yourself 15 minutes to attempt the questions. Work as quickly as you can.

Instructions

In some of the sentences over the page, one of the underlined words or phrases is incorrect in terms of English usage. No sentence has more than one error. If you find the error, choose the appropriate letter. If you find no error, choose the letter D. Place your answer in the box.

95

1. A   B
Of these dresses, I think this is the prettiest. Do you think
             C   D
this is the more prettier? No error

Answer

2.   A   B
Giving the ice cream to my sister and I, my father then got
   C   D
into the car. No error

Answer

3.   A   B
Of the two dogs that the family owns, the Labrador is the
      C   D
fatter. No error

Answer

4.   A   B

To who should I send this letter? I asked my boss, as I
  C   D

paused before his desk. No error

Answer

5. A   B   C

But is it right that these drugs should be proscribed; that
                                D

is, taken out of circulation? No error

Answer

6.   A   B

If you were to put fewer than five items in the shopping
             C

basket, you could go through the express check-out.
      D

No error

Answer

7.   A   B   C

In comparison <u>with</u> the <u>English</u>, <u>it is always said</u> that the

                                   D

Irish are more poetic. <u>No error</u>

Answer

8.   A   B

The line <u>managers</u> were advised that they should <u>council</u>

                                        C   D

their staff about the impending <u>take-over</u>. <u>No error</u>

Answer

9.   A

Since I had <u>learnt</u> to love her so much when she was alive,

             B   C   D

I now <u>treasure</u> my <u>mother's-in-law</u> picture. <u>No error</u>

Answer

10.   A   B   C
    The <u>1900s</u> <u>were</u> a time when many <u>Spanish-speaking</u>
                                    D
    immigrants arrived in the USA. <u>No error</u>

                                        Answer

11.   A   B
    There was scarcely <u>no one</u> in the room <u>to whom</u> I could
       C   D
    <u>have</u> entrusted my secret. <u>No error</u>

                                        Answer

12.   A   B
    <u>Taking</u> vitamins is a way of <u>insuring</u> long life, according to
                C   D
    the <u>current</u> thinking. <u>No error</u>

                                        Answer

13.
                A   B

Each of the <u>hotel's</u> 500 rooms <u>were</u> equipped with
                          C   D

televisions, baths, <u>kettles and</u> double beds. <u>No error</u>

Answer

14.
           A   B

<u>To do this gradually</u> must be the <u>best</u> tactic, as to do
                          C   D

otherwise would be to <u>jeopardise</u> the project. <u>No error</u>

Answer

15.
                      A   B

<u>Entering the house just before midnight,</u> <u>the broken glass</u>
                                  C   D

was discovered by my wife and <u>me</u>. <u>No error</u>

Answer

16.   A   B
     'How many <u>gin and tonics</u> would you be able to drink in an
               C   D
     evening?' <u>He</u> asked. <u>No error</u>

                                            Answer

17.
                                A
     Morphine and other <u>potentially</u> addictive drugs are valu-
                 B   C
     able <u>medically;</u> if abused, however <u>it</u> can cause untold
                      D
     damage. <u>No error</u>

                                              Answer

18.
                                        A
     According to the village gossip, the <u>local Vicar</u> had
            B   C
     <u>to be removed</u> from his post for <u>misappropriating</u> funds.
       D
     <u>No error</u>

                                            Answer

19.   A   B
    We've tried to deliberately stop arguing in front of the
                              C
    children because we have realised it disturbs them.
        D
    No error

                                        Answer

20.   A   B
    The following people could be said to have been successful
        C
    leaders: Margaret Thatcher, Churchill and Charles de
                  D
    Gaulle. No error

                                        Answer

21.   A   B
    The children's toys were still laying out on the table when
                          C   D
    the parents returned. No error

                                        Answer

22.   A   B

<u>Paula already left</u> by the time <u>I arrived</u> so I realised that
                         C

neither she nor I <u>was</u> going to get to the meeting in time.
       D

<u>No error</u>

Answer

23.   A   B

Every man, woman and child on the ship <u>is</u> able to fit <u>into</u>
                                          C

the lifeboat, so no one should fear for <u>his or her</u> life.
       D

<u>No error</u>

Answer

24.   A

<u>Which</u> of these two houses belongs to <u>you</u>? <u>Ours</u> is the
                           D

house on the left. <u>No error</u>

Answer

25.   A   B

<u>Us</u> women feel that we have suffered <u>too</u> much at the

  C   D

<u>hands</u> of men. <u>No error</u>

Answer

Answers to Chapter 4

Correct sentences (page 74)

1. = C
2. = B
3. = C
4. = A
5. = A
6. = A
7. = B. Note that family is a collective noun and should therefore take a singular verb.
8. = B
9. = A
10. = C

Incorrect sentences (page 78)

11. = C
12. = A
13. = C
14. = A
15. = D

Split infinitives (page 80)

16. = A
17. = C
18. = A
19. = C
20. = A
21. = B

Apostrophes (page 82)

22. = B,C
23. = A
24. = A, B
25. = A. Note that while 60's is often seen in print, this is not correct.
26. = D

Parts of a sentence (page 84)

27. = B
28. = D
29. = C
30. = C
31. = C

Use of negatives (page 87)

32. = A

Use of capitals (page 88)

33. = B,F,G

Incomplete sentences (page 89)

34. = A,C,D,E,F

Practice punctuation (page 89)

35. = A
36. = B
37. = A
38. = C
39. = A
40. = B
41. = B
42. = C
43. = C
44. = C

Common spelling mistakes (page 93)

45. You should have underlined numbers:
1, 2, 3, 4, 6 (this is US spelling), 8, 9, 11, 12, 14, 15, 16, 17, 19, 21, 22, 25, 26, 27, 28, 29, 30, 32, 34, 35, 36, 38, 42, 43, 44, 45

Choice of words (page 94)

46. You should have underlined the following words:

A	=	complimentary	I =	flaunt
B	=	effect	J =	take
C	=	continual	K =	from
D	=	advice	L =	fewer
E	=	all ready	M =	farther
F	=	among	N =	you
G	=	into	O =	lying
H	=	no word is required		

Mock test

1. = C	10. = D	19. = A
2. = A	11. = A	20. = D
3. = A	12. = B	21. = B
4. = A	13. = B	22. = A
5. = A	14. = D	23. = D
6. = D	15. = A	24. = D
7. = D	16. = C	25. = A
8. = B	17. = C	
9. = C	18. = A	

Chapter 5
Practice Business Judgement and Data Sufficiency

Business judgement and data sufficiency tests

At management and graduate levels it is common for tests to be formulated as exercises from which you have to select the appropriate data in order to answer the questions. Increasingly, employers use exercises which are relevant to the industry or even the job for which you have applied.

In some instances you are not required to work out the problem but to make an assessment of whether or not the data provided permit you to answer the question. Sometimes the data are presented in tabulated form.

In the following pages you will find practice exercises and questions, the aim of which is to allow you to develop a test strategy for this type of question. The practice will also allow you to build up speed and skill in the assimilation of data presented graphically.

Many of the questions do not require you to work out the answer, only to state whether or not sufficient data are provided for you to do so. So take care to ensure that you do not waste time doing unnecessary working out.

You will find the answers at the end of the chapter.

Practice questions

Situation 1

A factory is to commission two production lines. Production line 1 is to use existing technology. Production line 2 is to use the latest innovations in technology and, while promising to achieve considerable advances in productivity, it will take longer to install and is likely to experience teething problems. Graph 1 illustrates the productive record of each production line. Refer to the graph in order to answer the following questions.

Graph 1

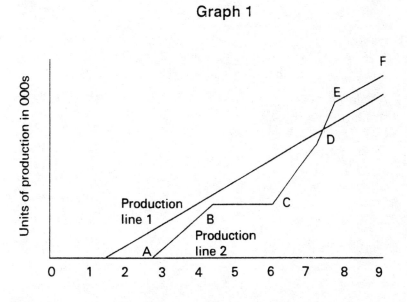

Month

Question 1
In which month did production line 2 overtake production line 1 in the total number of units produced?

Answer

Question 2

From the information given is it possible to attribute a reason why production line 1's record forms a straight line while production line 2's record takes the form of a polygon?

A = Yes, it is possible to attribute a reason
B = No, it is not possible to attribute a reason
C = You cannot tell if it is possible or not

Answer

Question 3

The manager of production line 2 reported a complete breakdown. At what point did this occur?

A Month 3
B During month 4
C Before month 4
D You cannot tell

Answer

Question 4

Consider the following questions (A and B) and indicate whether both, either or neither can be answered given the available data.

A Can the duration of the reported breakdown be established?

B Can the loss of production be quantified?

1. if both questions A and B can be answered
2. if only question A can be answered
3. if only question B can be answered
4. if neither question can be answered

Answer

Situation 2

Fifty candidates sat a test and the number of candidates who scored more than a specific number of correct answers is illustrated in graph 2. Refer to this graph in order to answer the following questions:

Graph 2

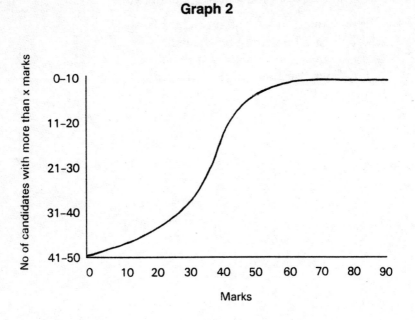

Question 5
What proportion of the candidates achieved over 50 correct marks?

A = The majority
B = A sizeable minority
C = Only a few
D = You cannot tell

Answer

Question 6
Is it possible to work out the median?

A = Yes, it is possible
B = No, it is not possible
C = You cannot tell if it is possible or not

Answer

Question 7
A curve such as the one drawn in graph 2 is called a:

A = Polygon
B = Ogive
C = Parallel
D = None of these

Answer

Question 8
Consider the following questions (A and B) and indicate whether both, either or neither can be answered given the available data.

A Did the 50 candidates do well or badly in the test?
B How many candidates got more than 70 marks out of 100?

1. if both questions A and B can be answered
2. if only question A can be answered
3. if only question B can be answered
4. if neither question can be answered

Answer

Situation 3

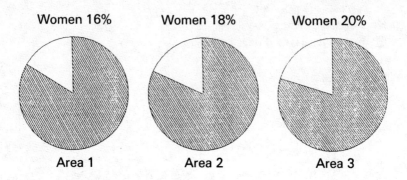

Women 16%

Women 18%

Women 20%

Area 1

Area 2

Area 3

The three pie charts demonstrate the level of unemployment among women as a percentage of the economically active population in three areas. The economically active population excludes both people too old or too young to work. The total economically active population for the three areas is 55,000.

Question 9
Is it possible to work out the percentage level of unemployment for the total populations of all three areas?

A = Yes, it is possible
B = No, it is not possible
C = You cannot tell if it is possible or not

Answer

Question 10

What is the mean percentage rate of unemployment for economically active women across the three areas?

A = 18%
B = 54%
C = 3%
D = You cannot tell

Answer

Question 11

How many unemployed women are there?

A = 22,500
B = More than half the total
C = Less than half the total
D = You cannot tell

Answer

Question 12

Consider the following questions (A and B) and indicate whether both, either or neither can be answered given the available data.

A Why are there more unemployed men than women?
B What is the total working population across the three areas?

1. if both questions A and B can be answered
2. if only question A can be answered
3. if only question B can be answered
4. if neither question can be answered

Answer

Situation 4

The gender of customers who requested childcare facilities at the shopping arcade.

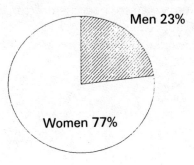

Men 23%

Women 77%

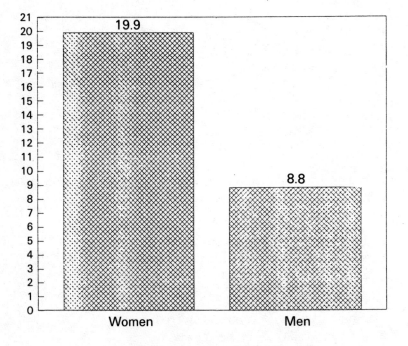

The percentage of customers wanting childcare facilities who were willing to pay for the service

The managers of a shopping arcade undertook a process of customer consultation and found that high on the list of facilities requested by customers was a shoppers' crèche. In total 800 customers took part in the survey which was conducted during working hours between Monday 14th and Wednesday 16th May.

Question 13
What percentage of women who requested childcare facilities were also willing to pay to use the service?

A = 19.9%
B = 23%
C = 77%
D = You cannot tell

Answer

Question 14
What percentage of male customers requested childcare facilities?

A = 77%
B = 8.8%
C = 23%
D = You cannot tell

Answer

Question 15

Is it true to say that 100 per cent of customers who took part in the survey wanted childcare facilities at the arcade?

A = Yes
B = No
C = You cannot tell

Answer

Question 16

Consider the following questions (A and B) and indicate whether both, either or neither can be answered given the available data.

A What is the ratio between men and women customers who wanted childcare facilities?
B How might the result have been affected had the management arranged for the survey to be carried out over a weekend rather than during the working week?

1. if both questions A and B can be answered
2. if only question A can be answered
3. if only question B can be answered
4. if neither question can be answered

Answer

Situation 5

The programmes director of a local radio station received the cohort (overleaf) which compares the age and gender of listeners. During the period to which the cohort refers, 52 per cent of the station's audience were women. Most mornings 125,000 families tune in for the breakfast show.

Use this information and the data contained in the cohort to answer the questions which follow.

Question 17
What percentage of male listeners are aged under 15 years?

A = 0–15%   Answer
B = Between 15 and 20%
C = Between 30 and 35%
D = You cannot tell

Question 18
What percentage of women aged between 16 and 24 years tune into the station?

A = Just under 15%   Answer
B = 20%
C = 100%
D = You cannot tell

Question 19
What percentage of women listeners are aged 45 years?

A = Just over 10%   Answer
B = Just under 10%
C = You cannot tell

Question 20

Consider the following questions and indicate whether both, either or neither can be answered given the available data.

A What percentage of listeners are aged between 25 and 39 years?

B With which age group is the station most popular?

Age/gender cohort of local radio station listeners

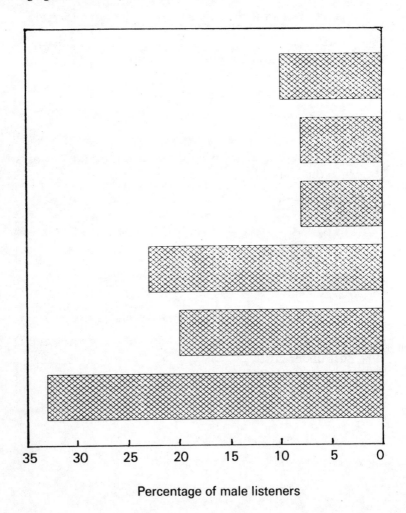

Percentage of male listeners

1. if both questions A and B can be answered
2. if only question A can be answered
3. if only question B can be answered
4. if neither question can be answered

Answer

Answers on page 123.

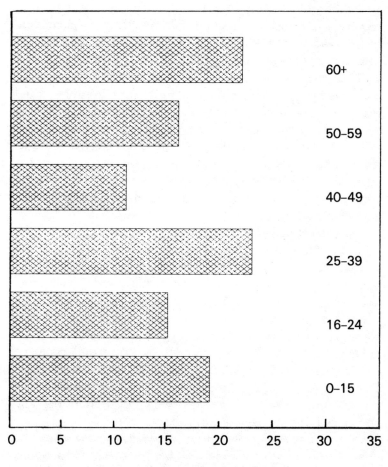

Percentage of female listeners

Chapter 6

Practice Reading Comprehension

Reading comprehension tests

At first sight reading comprehension tests may appear to require no advance preparation. We daily extract information from written sources and it is natural to assume that we therefore already possess the appropriate skills and will do well at these types of test.

However, our daily reading and interpretation of written material may fail to serve as sufficient preparation. This is because the tests may measure our ability in particular reading skills not practised in our daily reading. The tests may include, for example, questions about the logical sequence of the argument, or questions which expect the reader to identify the conclusions drawn from, or essential premisses to, an argument.

The subject matter of the passages used in reading comprehension tests is also likely to be unfamiliar. It may, for example, include technical data from engineering or science or a subject from the arts which draws on an unfamiliar and sophisticated vocabulary.

Practice in realistic reading comprehension exercises will allow you to develop a test strategy and achieve the necessary detailed reading under timed conditions. When undertaking a reading comprehension test it is far better to undertake a single detailed reading rather than have to refer back to the passage repeatedly. It often pays to read the questions first and then pick out the answers from the passage.

Do not allow your own prior knowledge or views on the subject to influence your answers. It is important to base your answers only on the content or implied content of the passage.

Over the page you will find three passages and 15 questions (five per passage) which relate to the passages.

Allow yourself 20 minutes to attempt the 15 questions. Do not turn the page until you are ready to begin the test. Answers are provided at the end of the chapter.

Answers to Chapter 5

1.	7	11.	D
2.	A	12.	3
3.	B	13.	A
4.	1	14.	C
5.	C	15.	B
6.	A	16.	2
7.	B	17.	C
8.	3	18.	A
9.	B	19.	C
10.	A	20.	1

Practice questions

Passage 1

He that is nourished by the acorns he picked up under an oak, or the apples he gathered from the trees in the wood, has certainly appropriated them to himself. Nobody can deny but the nourishment is his. I ask, then, when did they begin to be his? when he digested? or when he ate? or when he boiled? or when he brought them home? or when he picked them up? And it is plain, if the first gathering made them not his, nothing else could. That labour put a distinction between them and common. That added something to them more than Nature, the common mother of all, had done, and so they became his private right. . . .

His labour hath taken it out of the hands of Nature where it was common, and belonged equally to all her children, and hath thereby appropriated it to himself. . . .

It will, perhaps, be objected to this, that if gathering the acorns or other fruits of the earth, etc, makes a right to them, then any one may engross as much as he will. To which I answer, Not so. The same law of Nature that does by this means give us property, does also bound that property too. 'God has given us all things richly.' Is the voice of reason confirmed by inspiration? But how far has He given it us – 'to enjoy'? As much as any one can make use of to any advantage of life before it spoils, so much he may by his labour fix a property in. Whatever is beyond this is more than his share, and belongs to others. . . .

He who gathered as much of the wild fruit, killed, caught, or tamed as many of the beasts as he could – he that so employed his pains about any of the spontaneous products of Nature as any way to alter them from the state Nature put them in, by placing any of his labour on them, did thereby acquire a propriety in them; but if they perished in his possession without their due use – if the fruits rotted or the venison putrefied before he could spend it, he offended against the common law of Nature, and was liable to be punished: he invaded his neighbour's share, for he had no right farther than his use called for any of them, and they might serve to afford him conveniences of life.

John Locke, Section V, *An Essay Concerning the True Original, Extent and End of Civil Government* (1690)

Question 1
The primary purpose of the passage is to:

A Describe the way in which we lived before civilisation
B Promote the equal sharing of the world's scarce resources
C Investigate the basis for legitimate private property
D None of these

Answer

Question 2
The objection that Locke's argument allows one to 'engross as much as he will' fails because:

A God has given us all things richly so we can take as much as we like
B The fruit will rot and the venison will putrefy so there is no point taking more than you need
C The law of Nature dictates that if we take more than we can use we have taken something which belongs to others
D None of these

Answer

Question 3

Which of the following words describes the tone of the passage:

A Humorous?
B Contrived?
C Journalistic?
D None of these?

Answer

Question 4

Locke suggests that it is unequivocal that we have appropriated something for ourselves if we:

A Collected it and carried it away
B Have eaten and digested it
C Stored it for the winter
D None of these

Answer

Question 5

In the passage Locke argues that you can acquire something as your own property if you:

A Share it with others
B Inherit it
C Seize a neighbour's share
D None of these

Answer

Passage 2

The produce of labour constitutes the natural recompense or wages of labour.

In that original state of things, which precedes both the appropriation of land and the accumulation of stock, the whole produce of labour belongs to the labourer. He has neither landlord nor master to share with him.

Had this state continued, the wages of labour would have augmented with all those improvements in its productive powers, to which the division of labour gives occasion. All things would gradually have become cheaper. They would have been produced by a smaller quantity of labour; and as the commodities produced by equal quantities of labour would naturally in this state of things be exchanged for one another, they would have been purchased likewise with the produce of a small quantity.

But though all things would have become cheaper in reality, in appearance many things might have become dearer than before, or have been exchanged for a greater quantity of other goods. Let us suppose, for example, that in the greater part of employments the productive powers of labour had been improved to tenfold, or that a day's labour could produce ten times the quantity of work which it had done originally; but that in a particular employment they had been improved only to double, or that a day's labour could produce only twice the quantity of work which it had done before. In exchanging the produce of a day's labour in the greater part of employments, for that of a day's labour in this particular one, ten times the original quantity of work in them would purchase only twice the original quantity in it. Any particular quantity in it, therefore, a pound weight, for example, would appear to be five times dearer than before. In reality, however, it would be twice as cheap. Though it required five times the quantity of other goods to purchase it, it would require only half the quantity of labour either to purchase or to produce it. The acquisition, therefore, would be twice as easy as before.

Adam Smith, Of the Wages of Labour, Chapter VIII, Volume 1, *The Wealth of Nations* (1776)

Question 1

The passage addresses which of the following issues:

A The effect of the division of labour on productive power
B The effect on prices if labourers were to keep all the product of their labour
C The effect on prices if labourers kept all the product of their labour and their labour benefited from improvements in productive power
D None of these

Answer

Question 2

If labourers were to keep all the product of their labour, Smith states that things would become cheaper in:

A Reality
B Appearance
C The market-place
D None of these

Answer

Question 3
If the productive power of labour is improved tenfold, Smith claimed:

A Things would appear five times cheaper
B Things would in reality be twice as cheap
C Things would appear five times dearer
D None of these

Answer

Question 4
Smith holds that commodities would continue to be exchanged in equal quantities only if:

A One product benefited more from improvements in productive power than the other
B Labour was divided, land appropriated and stock accumulated
C Both products benefited equally from improvements in productive power
D None of these

Answer

129

Question 5
According to Smith, while in reality things would become cheaper in appearance:

A All things would become dearer
B Some things would become dearer
C Some things might become dearer
D None of these

Answer

Passage 3

Now suppose that the average amount of the daily necessaries of a labouring man require six hours of average labour for their production. Suppose, moreover, six hours of average labour to be also realised in a quantity of gold equal to three shillings. Then three shillings would be the Price, or the monetary expression of the Daily Value of that man's Labouring Power. If he worked daily six hours he would daily produce a value sufficient to buy the average amount of his daily necessaries, or to maintain himself as a labouring man.

But our man is a wages labourer. He must, therefore, sell his labouring power to a capitalist. If he sells it at three shillings daily, or 18 shillings weekly, he sells it at its value. Suppose him to be a spinner. If he works six hours daily he will add to the cotton a value of three shillings daily. This value, daily added by him, would be an exact equivalent for the wages, or the price of his labouring power, received daily. But in that case no surplus value or surplus produce whatever would go to the capitalist. Here, then, we come to the rub. . . .

The value of the labouring power is determined by the quantity of labour necessary to maintain or reproduce it, but the use of that labouring power is only limited by the active energies and physical strength of the labourer. . . . Take the example of our spinner. We have seen that, to daily reproduce his labouring power, he must daily reproduce a value of three shillings, which he will do by working six hours daily. But this does not disable him from working ten or twelve or more hours a day. But by paying the daily or weekly value of the spinner's labouring power, the capitalist has acquired the right of using that labouring power during the whole day or week. He will, therefore, make him work say, daily, twelve hours. Over and above the six hours required to replace his wages, or the value of his labouring power, he will, therefore, have to work six other hours, which I shall call hours of surplus labour, which surplus labour will realise itself in a surplus value and a surplus produce. If our spinner, for example, by his daily labour of six hours, added three shillings' value to the cotton, a value forming an exact equivalent to his wages, he will, in twelve hours, add six shillings' worth to the cotton, and produce a proportional surplus of yarn. As he has sold his labouring power to the capitalist, the whole value or produce created by him belongs to the capitalist, the owner ... of his labouring power.

Karl Marx, Production of Surplus Value, Section VIII, *Wages, Price and Profit* (1865)

Question 1
Marx holds that 'the rub' is:

A That the spinner sells his labouring power at its value
B That the spinner works a 12-hour day
C That the spinner's surplus value goes to the capitalist
D None of these

Answer

Question 2
With which of the following ideas would the author probably agree?

A Industrial profit is a legitimate part of the value of a commodity
B Industrial profit is only a different name for the unpaid labour enclosed in a commodity
C If wages fall, profits fall; if wages rise, profits will rise
D None of these

Answer

Question 3

Identify from the following a correct restatement of the main idea of the passage:

A The amount of surplus value depends on the ratio in which the working day is prolonged over the time it takes for the working man to replace his wages
B A general rise in the rate of wages would result in a fall in the general rate of profit
C It is the constant tendency of capitalists to stretch the working day to its utmost physically possible length
D None of these

Answer

Question 4

Which of the following statements best describes the approach taken by Marx in the passage?

A He refutes a stated view
B He sets out to be expansive
C His objective is to compare and contrast
D None of these

Answer

Question 5
According to Marx the spinner's daily necessities require:

A Three shillings
B Six hours of average labour
C A twelve-hour working day
D None of these

Answer

Answers on page 136.

Further Reading

Great Answers to Tough Interview Questions, 3rd edition, Martin John Yate (Kogan Page, 1992)

How to Pass Selection Tests, Mike Bryon and Sanjay Modha (Kogan Page, 1991)

How to Succeed in Psychometric Tests, David Cohen (Sheldon, 1993)

How to Win at Aptitude Tests, Paul Pelshenke (Thorsons, 1993)

Successful Interview Skills, Rebecca Corfield, (Kogan Page, 1992)

Test Your Own Aptitude, 2nd edition, Jim Barrett and Geoff Williams (Kogan Page, 1990)

Your Employment Rights, Michael Malone (Kogan Page, 1992)

In the Macmillan Work Out series:

The fundamental rules of arithmetic:
Numeracy, F E Penkeith

For exercises and explanations at A level:
Applied Mathematics and *Pure Mathematics*, both by Roger Haines and Betty Haines

Answers to reading comprehension questions in Chapter 6

Passage 1

1. C
2. C
3. B

4. B
5. D

Passage 2

1. C
2. A
3. D

4. C
5. C

Passage 3

1. C
2. B
3. A

4. B
5. B